cribed to William Hendry

Brother James's Air

(Marosa)

Arranged for mixed voices by
GORDON JACOB

Brother James is the familiar name by which many remember the late James Leith Macbeth Bain, and this Air is perhaps the most beautiful of many that came to him spontaneously.

Score and parts for strings are available on hire. A version for S.S.A. is also on sale (OCS 558).

Printed in Great Britain

OXFORD UNIVERSITY PRESS, MUSIC DEPARTMENT, GREAT CLARENDON STREET, OXFORD OX2 6DP

XFORD CHORAL SONGS

:S 763

xed voices

Brother James's Air

(Marosa)

Arranged for mixed voices by

Gordon Jacob

MUSIC DEPARTMENT

OXFORD
UNIVERSITY PRESS

makes me down to lie in pastures green, He leadeth me The
me to walk doth make With - in the Paths of Blessedness, E'en
makes me down to lie in pastures green, He leadeth me The
me to walk doth make With - in the Paths of Blessedness, E'en
makes me down to lie in pastures green, He leadeth me The
me to walk doth make With - in the Paths of Blessedness, E'en
makes me down to lie in pastures green, He leadeth me The
me to walk doth make With - in the Paths of Blessedness, E'en
qui - et wa - ters by. He lead - eth me, He
for His own Name's sake. With - in the Paths of
qui - et wa - ters by. He lead - eth me, He
for His own Name's sake. With - in the Paths of
qui - et wa - ters by. He lead - eth me, He
for His own Name's sake. With - in the Paths of
qui - et wa - ters by. He lead - eth me, He
for His own Name's sake. With - in the Paths of

D.C.
lead - eth me, The qui - et wa - ters by.
Bless - ed - ness, E'en for His own Name's sake.
D.C.
lead - eth me, The qui - et wa - ters by.
Bless - ed - ness, E'en for His own Name's sake.
D.C.
lead - eth me, The qui - et wa - ters by.
Bless - ed - ness, E'en for His own Name's sake.
D.C.
lead - eth me, The qui - et wa - ters by.
Bless - ed - ness, E'en for His own Name's sake.
D.C.

p
Yea, though I pass thro' shadowed vale, Yet will I fear no
p
Yea, though I pass thro' shadowed vale, Yet will I fear no
mf
Yea, though I pass thro' shadowed vale, Yet will I fear no
mf
Yea, though I pass thro' shadowed vale, Yet will I fear no
marc.

ill; For Thou art with me, And Thy Rod and Staff me com - fort
ill; For Thou art with me, And Thy Rod and Staff me com - fort
ill; For Thou art with me, And Thy Rod and Staff me com - fort
ill; For Thou art with me, And Thy Rod and Staff me com - fort
mf
still. Thy Rod and Staff me comfort still, me com - fort
mf
still. Thy Rod and Staff me comfort still, me com - fort
still. Thy Rod and Staff me com - fort
still. Thy Rod and Staff me com - fort

mp
still. My ta-ble Thou hast fur-nish-ed In presence of my
p
still. Ah
p
still. Ah Ah
p
still. Ah
foes; My head with oil Thou dost a-noint, And my cup o - ver -
Ah
Ah Ah
Ah

- flows. My head Thou dost with oil a-noint, And my cup o - ver -
My head Thou dost with oil a-noint, And my cup o - ver -
My head Thou dost with oil a-noint, And my cup o - ver -
My head Thou dost with oil a-noint, And_ my cup o - ver -

f
- flows. 5 Good - ness and mer - cy all my days Will sure-ly fol - low
- flows. 5 Good - ness and mer - cy_ all my days Will sure-ly fol - low
- flows. 5 Good - ness and mer - cy all my days Will sure-ly fol - low
- flows. 5 Good - ness and mer - cy all my days Will sure-ly fol - low
f

ISBN 0-19-340524-5

£1.85

Reproduced and printed by
Halstan & Co. Ltd., Amersham, Bucks., England